Making and Keeping Friends" is a road map to change, to attain the wonderful and self-fulfilling relationships of friendship. It is easy to follow, and a clear guide for those who are motivated to improve their social skills. It addresses the psychological, social, emotional and trust elements as they relate to making and keeping friends. I have seen how Linda Thalheimer has greatly improved the self-esteem, communication skills, and development of trust, nurturing the endearing qualities of those needing and wanting long-lasting social skills. She shares her techniques in this remarkable book.

Robert A. Weaver III, Ph.D.,
Director and Neuropsychologist

Dr. Weaver (a.k.a. Buck) is a psychologist and neuropsychologist in Wayland, MA. He developed the strength-based Weaver Center over 30 years ago, with a specialty in adolescents and young adults.

INTERACTIVE GUIDE

TO

MAKING & KEEPING FRIENDS

INTERACTIVE GUIDE TO MAKING & KEEPING FRIENDS

Linda Thalheimer OTR/L, MHA
and
Lau Lapides Company
Media, Photography,Videography,
& Voice Over Production Team

ISBN: 978-1-6653-0659-1 - Paperback
eISBN: 978-1-6653-0660-7 - eBook

These ISBNs are the property of BookLogix for the express purpose of sales and distribution of this title. BookLogix is not responsible for the writing, editing, or design/appearance of this book. The content of this book is the property of the copyright holder only. BookLogix does not hold any ownership of the content of this book and is not liable in any way for the materials contained within. The views and opinions expressed in this book are the property of the Author/ Copyright holder, and do not necessarily reflect those of BookLogix.

♾ This paper meets the requirements of ANSI/NISO Z39.48-1992 (Permanence of Paper)

Credit for photographs & videos given to Lau Lapides Company

0 7 1 1 2 3

Dedication

I dedicate this book to my niece, Marissa, who no matter what the obstacles, keeps trying to be a better person and a better friend. When I think back to when she entered college, unable to even communicate a problem through hysterical tears of anxiety, and see her now, a college graduate, married, the mother of two beautiful children, and a mentor to the Friends' Group, I couldn't be prouder.

Marissa was the motivation for The Friends Group, a group that brings together young adults who want to make and keep friends.

Thank you to the members of The Friends Group for helping me appreciate the impact of anxiety on self-esteem and processing and how quickly change can be made amongst friends. Thank you for your acceptance, kindness, and support of each other; personifying the word "friendship".

Table of Contents

INTRODUCTION

Friends are important, whether it be for companionship to share similar interests and activities or to share your thoughts and emotions. At the very least, a friend is someone you like and can trust so that when you call with an invitation to get together, you know, if at all possible, the answer will be yes. The more you want out of a friendship, the more complicated the skills are to meet and keep such friends.

Everyone, at one time or another, feels alone. Even those that we may believe are the most confident, teachers, musicians, comedians, actors, and even clergy, can feel very much alone when they walk off the stage. Feeling alone is a common feeling. Feeling alone is not the same as being alone. One can feel very content and happy by oneself and even crave alone time. There are times we may want to be alone, and other times we want to be with others and feel appreciated, wanted, and part of a group. When we are left out of a group invite or feel unincluded while in a group, this is when we feel most lonely.

We all want a good friend. Without a friend, we can be overcome by loneliness, causing sadness and low self-esteem. This prevents us from even trying, leading to an endless loop of aloneness. This book is designed to help you understand how to make that first impression so that people can get to know the real you.

It is also intended to help you continue a relationship by understanding social cues, communication strategies as well as appropriate boundaries.

While we want others to like us for who we are, it is also important to know that first impressions count. If we don't make a good first impression, we may never get a chance to communicate who we really are and lose the opportunity to make a new friend. It is also important to know that some of our automatic actions and behaviors may be interpreted as something other than their intention or lack of intention. These false interpretations may interfere with other's interest in getting to know you better.

Once you make a friend, it is equally important to know how to cultivate that relationship and which actions may "scare" away new acquaintances. Trying to overcome continual rejection often leads one to accept "friends" who encourage us to do what we know is not right, such as smoking, doing drugs, stealing, or even participating in extreme cult-like groups. This is understandable, but must be seen for the dangers it represents. Friendship is such an important part of our lives. When people make you feel wanted, important and part of a group with a common goal, it feels good. But it's important to be able to remain objective and know that these people are not real friends.

We may assume that making friends comes naturally but, in fact, it is a skill; a skill that can be learned. To be successful, one only needs to want friendship enough to be willing to try to learn and practice new strategies and to be open to challenging oneself and accepting constructive feedback.

Linda Thalheimer

OTR/L, MHA

How to Use This Interactive Book

The chapters are set up with skills and a pattern for learning.

Each chapter:
1. Identifies a skill or a problem.
2. Explains how the skill or the problem may be perceived by others.
3. Illustrates each skill or problem.
4. Provides practice activities to get better at the skill or minimize the problem
5. Visit & subscribe to our YouTube channel to take advantage of the videos included with this book as well as future content!
   Channel: @makingandkeepingfriends

It is a good idea to check out each chapter. If you already have the skill or don't have the problem identified in the chapter, continue to the next chapter.

Read over the chapters, listen and practice those chapters that relate the most to your need for skills development.

Remember, no matter how long you have had a habit, it only takes two weeks to change if you are motivated and practice!

Getting Started

Many of us have experienced rejection so many times, we don't even want to try anymore. But this time, it will be different. Perception is everything. For example, two people can get on an airplane. One person is excited to be flying in the clouds and the person in the very next seat can be terrified that the plane will crash. The only difference is each individual's perception of the situation. Trying new things often feels uncomfortable. Instead of aniticpating anxiety, think of making friends as playing a part in which you are confident. As you understand each of the steps, you will become more aware of your abilities and the more confident you will feel.

"The fastest way to change yourself is to hang out with the people who are already the way you want to be." Reid Hoffman, influencer, entrepreneur. When you are feeling desperate to make friends, you may settle for friends that are a bad influence. This quote is important to keep in mind so that you don't choose to hang out with people who you do not want to become.

The more confident you become, the easier it is to make friends. The easier it is to make friends, the greater the opportunity to choose your friends.

Playing the Part

You may have heard, that you have 3 seconds to get someone's attention on the internet before they will scroll to another page. It's not that much different in person. People will often make a decision in seconds if they want to invest more time in developing a friendship. Therefore, it is important to prepare for meeting new people.

General Guidelines:

1. Always be neat and clean. Even among friends, having hair clean and neat is a sign of respect.
2. Dress for the event. You can still maintain your individuality while dressing for a meeting. It is always better to be a little overdressed than underdressed for an event.
3. Wear a smile. Smiles are welcoming and portray a sense of confidence. People prefer to be with people who are happy and confident. It is also harder to be anxious while wearing a smile.

4. Be aware of the volume of how people are speaking. Speak at the same volume or even a little softer. Loud voices in a new setting are not typically welcomed.

5. Listening, more than speaking, is a good starting rule, as long as it is being perceived you are truly listening. This is enhanced by eye contact.

6. Be prepared to respond with questions to keep the conversation going. Generally, people like to talk about themselves.

7. Two things never to ask new acquaintances: how much they make or how much they weigh. Stay away from highly controversial subjects.

Most importantly, don't talk badly about other people. It tells the person that if you talk badly about others you are not trustworthy and could just as easily talk badly about them.

Eye Contact...

Eye contact says:
- I am interested.
- I am focused on what you are saying.
- I am not being distracted by other things.
- I am sincere.

Does eye contact make you feel uncomfortable? Unfortunately, lack of eye contact makes others feel uncomfortable.

Lack of eye contact says:
- I am not interested.
- I am distracted.
- I am bored.
- I am anxious.
- I am uncomfortable with this conversation.

Without good eye contact, it is difficult to make a connection with another person. Connections are necessary to make friends.

Eye Contact
Observe how the lack of eye contact makes
the other person feel uncomfortable. See how
a simple reminder to maintain eye contact
enables the two people to connect.

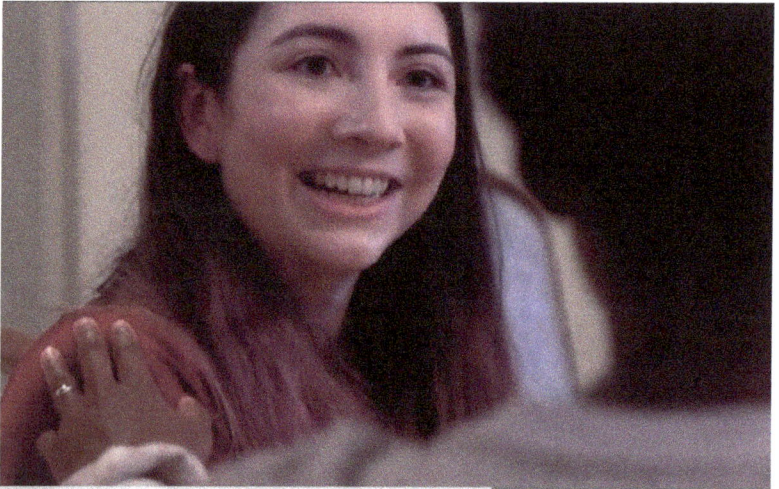

Visit YouTube to watch the video!
@makingandkeepingfriends

Eye Contact...

Practice Activity

Practice with a sibling, a parent or the next person with whom you are engaging in conversation.

1. Let this person know you are working on developing your eye contact skills.
2. Ask them to tell you every time your eyes veer away.
3. How many times did your partner tell you that you were looking away?
4. Try to maintain your eye contact for the majority of the conversation.

Which set of friends are connecting with good eye contact?

Managing Anxiety...

Anxiety can prevent us from trying new things and meeting new people. Without meeting new people, there is little potential to making new friends.

Anxiety doesn't just prevent us from meeting new people but it slows our mental processing. It can impair our ability to keep up with a conversation or create difficulty finding words to respond in conversation.

Anxiety can present itself as unwanted repetitive habits that make other people uncomfortable.

It is important to know, most people are not as confident as they appear. Pretending to be confident is much more common than you would expect.

How do you pretend to be confident?
1.Wear a smile
2.Maintain good eye contact
3.Control anxiety behaviors

Pretending to be confident helps one to feel more confident. Anxiety may feel so strong that it is difficult even to pretend. First you will need to become aware of what and when you experience uneasiness or anxiety. Awareness of your anxiety behaviors is a good first clue that you are becoming anxious. Make a plan of how to handle anticipated situations that cause anxiety. This will allow you to gain more confidence with your family, employer and/or teachers. As you start feeling more confident in your day to day practices, you will feel more confident with unanticipated situations when meeting and speaking with classmates/coworkers and potential new friends.

There will always be situations that create anxiety. For some people, if the anxiety is not controlled, anxiety behaviors may begin to snowball into what some describe as "snapping" which results in an extreme or potentially dangerous behavior. Before one "snaps", and becomes unable to process any more information, there are **many** things that can be done. Loss of control **never** needs to take place.

Whether it be a manager or a teacher, it is important they understand how you learn and process information. If you are someone who requires rules to be clearly detailed or demonstrated for you to effectively perform without anxiety or if you are someone who thinks more literally, has a compulsive need to complete a task or gets anxious when rules are changed or broken, then it may be helpful to have an advocate work with you and your manager or teacher together to make the work/school environment optimal for everyone. An advocate may be a professional counselor or anyone you trust that understands you, that can communicate on your behalf.

It is important to identify which rules are actually guidelines and those that are unbreakable rules, who in the workplace/school has the authority to change these rules and when there is more than one authority figure, whose rules should be prioritized to follow. An advocate may be helpful clarifying these rules, as well.

If you work in a store or restaurant, be prepared with a plan in mind because it is just a matter of time before you get overwhelmed with a difficult customer. If there is a manager on duty, call them as soon as you start feeling anxious; don't wait until it feels overwhelming. If there is no manager on duty, make sure you have created business cards with their name and phone number that you keep close by. When you find you are in a situation you cannot resolve, you hand them the business card and say, "I am sorry I can't help you, Please call my manager."

If for some reason, there is no one to call, then you politely ask the person to leave. If that person does not leave, you let them know you will call the police. If they don't leave, then call the police. There is no time in this process for anxiety to get out of control and, therefore, "hurtful" behaviors are not triggered.

The key to handling anxiety is to identify what situations make you most anxious.
1. Was it when you got lost?
2. Was it in a confrontation with a co-worker, boss, family member, or fellow student?
3. Was it when you felt misunderstood?

Kids can and will be mean. It may provide a little consolation to know that kids are often mean because of their own insecurities. They tend to choose to be with others similar to themselves, reinforcing their own value, aligning against others who are less similar. Unfortunately, middle schoolers tend to be the most extreme in this behavior.

"Popular" rarely means "nice". Find group activities that are more inclusive and less competitive such as the arts and those that engage in volunteer activities. If you are on a sports team, look for the other members of the team who have similar levels of skills.

Each time you try a new situation, ask yourself, "Was I happy with the outcome of the situation?" If not, "What could I have done differently to have had a better outcome?" Then try again in a different way, possibly in a different situation.

Discussing options with family members or counselors may be helpful to identify alternative ways to handle situations to have a better, less stressful outcome. Each time you address a challenging situation objectively, the greater your potential to have a better outcome and increase your confidence.

Practice Activities

1. Practice a calming exercise such as CALM. Identify a word that begins with each letter "C" for example "cat", and then "A" and then "L" and then "M". This will slow your mind down and give you time to process.
2. Identify an emergency call system of several people to call when you are in a challenging situation so that if one is not available there is another to fall back on.
3. Work with an advocate to help your teacher or employer understand your learning style and needs to make the environment work better for everyone.
4. Always be clear on the rules and to whom you report. Be clear on who can change the rules and the order of authority.
5. Make sure you have access to a person of authority when situations go wrong, whether it be a manager's cell phone or a set of cards (that you can make yourself) with the manager's name and number for quick access or to give to a customer.

Anxiety Behaviors...

Most of us have an anxiety habit. If you are trying to project confidence, you will want to eliminate your anxiety habit. The closer the habit is to the face, the greater the distraction. Anxiety habits are generally distracting to the conversation and negatively impact first impressions. Depending upon when they are displayed, they may also be interpreted as boredom.

Anxiety habits may include:
- Rubbing one's eyes, cheeks, chin, teeth, or ears
- Biting one's nails or cuticles
- Making repetitive facial movements
- Twisting or rubbing one's hair
- Avoiding eye contact

Less distractive anxiety habits may include:
- Fiddling with silverware or a pen
- Talking too quickly or not at all
- Rubbing or pinching one's arms
- Twiddling fingers in the lap

Anxiety behaviors
How do they make you feel? Would it be
challenging to hold a conversaton while
watching these behaviors?

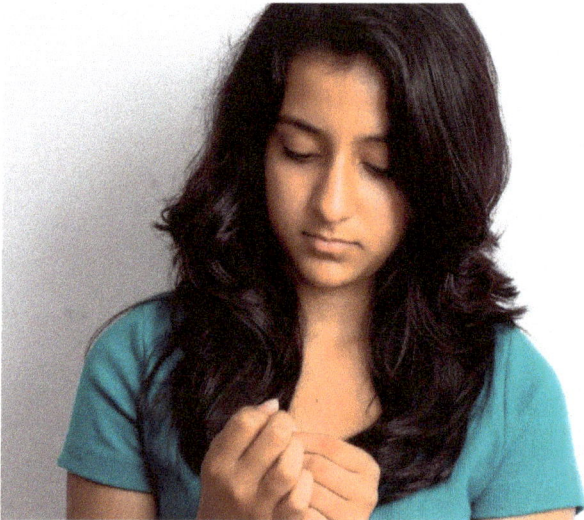

Visit YouTube to watch the video!
@makingandkeepingfriends

20

Do you have an anxiety habit?

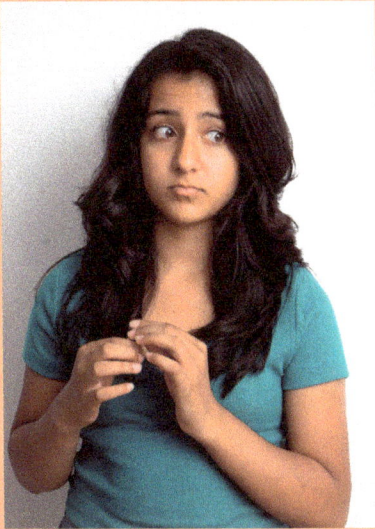

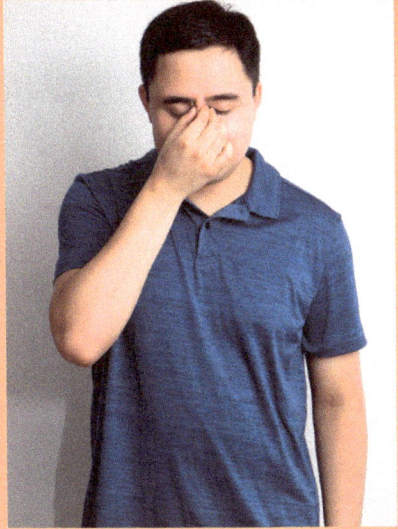

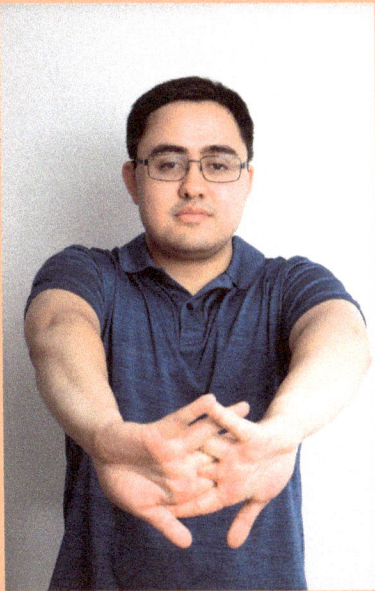

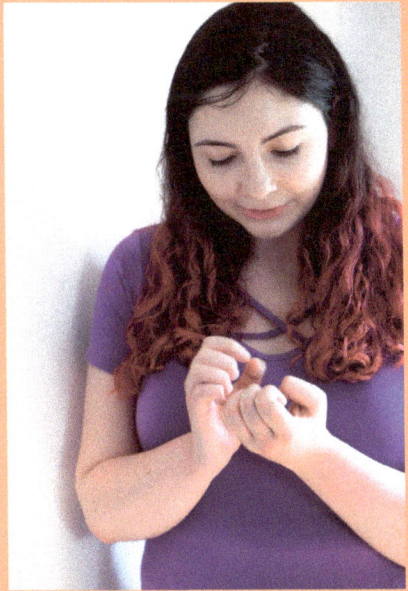

Practice Activity

1. Identify your anxiety habit.
2. Try to find out what triggers your anxiety habit.
3. Are you aware of when you are engaging in the habit?
   a. If not, ask for help. Tell your "helper", that every time you start the behavior, to give you a clue for you to stop or modify your behavior. This can be a shake of the head, or a clasping of the hands together as a visual clue for you to stop or clasp your hands into your lap.
4. Feel free to substitute other less distracting anxiety behaviors such as twirling a straw or spoon (a safe utensil). If possible, twiddling fingers in one lap out of sight is always better. Any substitute behavior needs to allow you and the other person to maintain eye contact which means you can't be looking at your hands.
5. Once successful at eliminating anxiety behaviors understand that in high-stress situations, these behaviors can return. You need to be aware so that you can calm yourself and present the best you.

Communication

Nonverbal communication is a way of telling someone about your feelings without words. It includes facial expressions, eye movements, and head, arm, leg, or full-body movements.

Why is this important? Non-verbal communication can be more important than words themselves. Someone may say "I'm having a great time.", but if they are fidgety and their eyes are wandering, they are more likely bored.

Clues that people are happy and interested in you and the conversation:
- They are smiling.
- They are maintaining eye contact.
- They are facing you directly.

Clues that people are getting bored:
- They stop smiling.
- Eyes are no longer keeping contact.
- They start to look away or around the room.
- They start to fidget.
- There is more body movement, (shifting weight in their feet).
- They may rotate their body away from you.

It is best not to start new conversations with highly controversial subjects, such as politics. It is easily possible to say something that makes another person uncomfortable or with which the other person does not agree. Therefore, it is important for you to be able to recognize the non-verbal clues of discomfort or frustration so that you can ask a question or change the subject. There is no need to continue a conversation when the other person is no longer engaging.

Clues that the person is getting frustrated or uncomfortable:
- Facial features will get tighter, and lips drew down a little.
- Eyes may divert from yours, or look up at the ceiling and then back.
- They may cross their arms, create a fist even if down by their side or grab one of their own wrists.
- They may change their stance to create more space between you.

Non-verbal Communication
Can you identify the emotion being expressed?

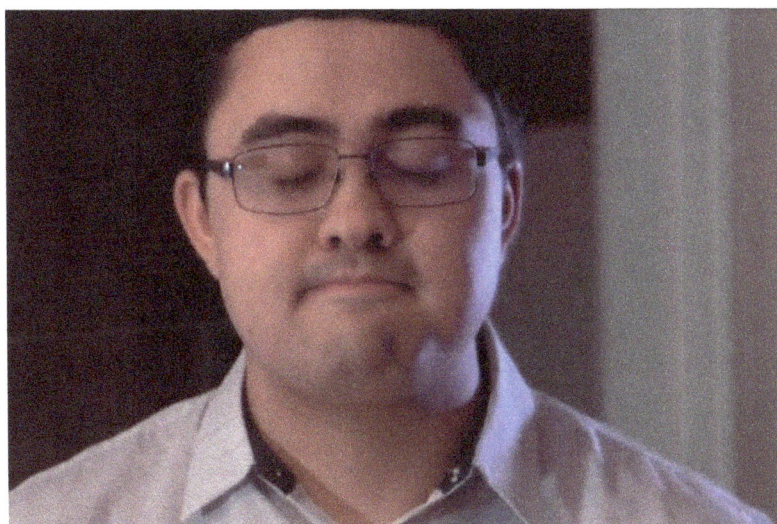

Visit YouTube to watch the video!
@makingandkeepingfriends

Practice Activities

1. On the next page are examples of how body language is a guide for whether to join in on a conversation. Next time you are in a group setting, try to recognize which sets of people are using body language to let you know they are interested in having you join and when they are not.

2. Watch TV with the sound off and try to guess the actor's mood based on facial expression and body language: happy, angry, shy, fearful, or sad.

   a. For example: While watching The Big Bang Theory, see if you can guess when Sheldon's friends are angry or frustrated with him. It happens frequently in this show.

   b. Check with a relative and see if you are right.

3. Practice in a mirror your own facial expressions. When you are happy, are you wearing a smile? This is the most important non-verbal clue to master.

Which group should you join?

The two in the front of the picture are making it very clear between their eye contact and their body langage, they don't want anyone disturbing their conversation.

Now the two in the front are making it clear, they are interested in including a third. Their bodies have rotated outwards to include another person. Their gaze is more flexible looking away from their partner.

Intonation

You may have heard the expression, "It's not what you say but how you say it that counts." Intonation is the rhythm and rise and fall of the voice. Intonation is important to the understanding of the true meaning of a sentence in a conversation. Using intonation, in combination with facial expressions and other non-verbal clues, gives you an even greater understanding about the meaning of a sentence than the words themselves.

Sarcasm is a form of communication, based on intonation. For someone who does not recognize the importance of tone, sarcasm will sound hurtful or like a lie, when actually, it is meant as a joke. For example, one might say, "I'm disappointed in you." right after you did something well. Or they might say "nice job" right after you did something poorly. Without listening to the tone of the sentence, the words will not make sense.

People may say words that are "mean" or "degrading", but with your ability to recognize intonation and facial expression, you can interpret that these are in fact friendly jokes, often poking fun at strong, quality characteristics. Statements such as "you are such a dork" or "a geek" are not necessarily intended as an insult. Generally, people who say this are a little jealous of the fact that you may be well-read or really smart. They are more likely "teasing" you than insulting you. (This is where texting can get people in trouble as there is no way to interpret the tone and intention of a statement.)

Intonation is also important to communicate how you feel about others or an activity. As you will hear in the video, monotone language implies a lack of interest.   Generally, we want to put emphasis on what is important in the sentence. For example, "Thanks, I had a good time" or "That was fun." Even when we can't hear the words, intonation can communicate if one is happy, interested, having fun, distracted or bored.

Intonation is important in communicating how you feel and to creates more interest while you are talking.

Intonation
Can you tell when the person is being sincere or sarcastic? Can you hear the difference between monotone and expressive?

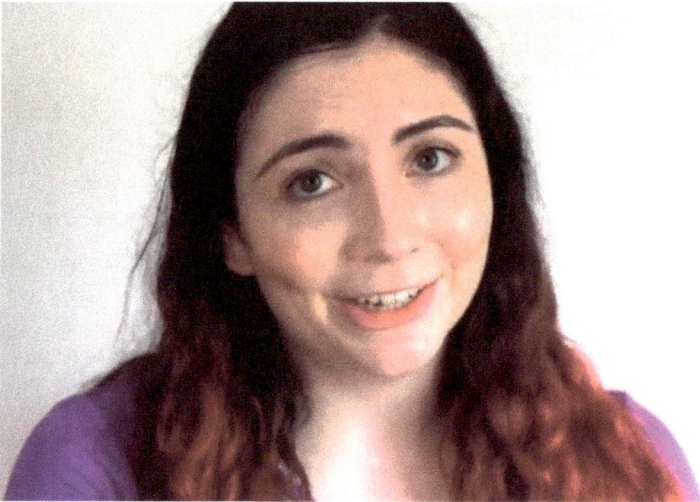

Visit YouTube to watch the video!
@makingandkeepingfriends

Practice Activities

1. Watch TV with a family member. Close your eyes and listen to the actors. Try to guess if the actors are happy, bored, sad, or angry. Ask your family member if you are right.
2. Read a book out loud with a family member. Take turns reading it with intonation from the characters' points of view.
3. Make a recording of yourself reading a story and see if you can make it sound interesting with your intonation.
4. When you are having conversations, try to be more aware of how you are feeling, and try to convey that in the tone of your sentences. It's always helpful to practice with people you trust.

Meal Time Social Skills...

Most social activities include food, whether it is a formal meal or buffet. There are two parts to social skills during mealtime: the act of eating and the art of communication. We will address them one at a time.

In addition to managing eye contact and controlling your anxiety behaviors, there are several more important social skills to master while eating.

No reaching across the table.
- You should not be getting out of your chair to reach for something or cross another person's body.
- When you need an item on the table, you need to ask someone to pass it to you.
- If the person next to you can help, you can touch them lightly on the arm to get their attention and say "Excuse me, would you please pass...".
- If someone is engaged in conversation or across the table, say, "Excuse me, would you please pass the ..." It is ok to interrupt the

conversation to ask for someone to pass something if the conversation is likely to last awhile.

- No dipping in group sauces. No eating from shared dishes.
  - Pour some sauce and/or take a portion of the shared dish onto your plate. You can always go back for more but always eat from your own plate.
  - Remember, if it requires a reach, make sure to ask that it be passed to you.
- Take small bites; no food should be hanging from your mouth.
  - It is disturbing and distracting to watch someone try to get food into their mouth because they took too large a bite.
  - Large bites also lead to chewing with your mouth open.
- Chew with your mouth closed.
  - Most of the time you won't recognize whether you eat with your mouth open or closed as it has become such a habit. Videotaping yourself with your phone is a good way to know for sure.
- Make sure your face is clear of food.
  - It's a good idea to wipe your mouth every so often, especially when eating foods with sauces and dressing.
- No picking your teeth.
  - It is not uncommon to get food stuck in your teeth and it is uncomfortable. As tempting as it is to just pick it out, you need to excuse yourself and fix the problem in the restroom, and then return.
- Never talk with food in your mouth.

Meal Time Social Skills
Can you identify which behaviors need to be modified?

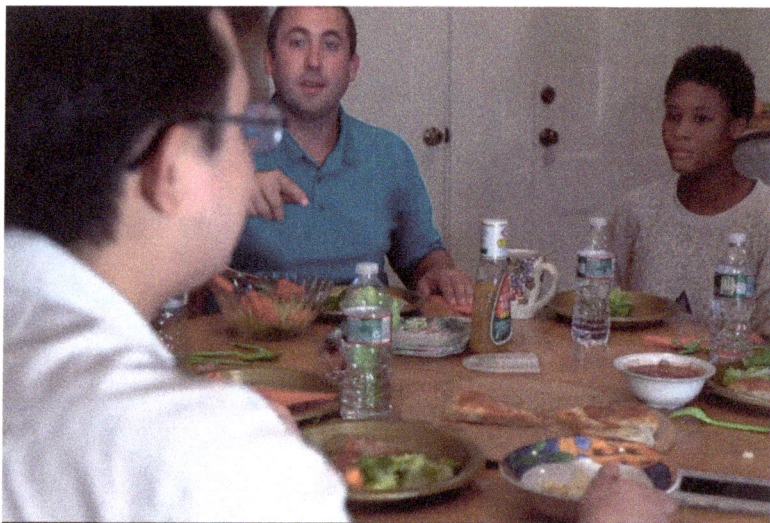

Visit YouTube to watch the video!
@makingandkeepingfriends

Dinner Time Conversation

- Before starting to talk, listen to hear if someone else is talking at the table already.
  - If someone is talking, you need to listen until they are done.
- Make sure you are looking towards the person who is talking.
  - This makes it easier to hear what they are saying and shows you are interested.
  - When the person is done speaking, you can ask them a question about the topic to continue the conversation, tell them about a similar experience or change the subject.
  - Even if others start to talk badly about others, you should not. It feels good to join in, but this will not reflect well on you and likely come back to haunt you.

- If no one is talking, this is the time for one of your conversation starters.
  - You can tell a short story about something that happened to you or something fun you did that week.
  - Try not to tell more than one story before another person tells one. The conversation should be back and forth.
  - Or you can start with a question to get others talking at the table

Here are a few conversation starters:
- Have you done anything fun or exciting lately?
- What was the last good book you read or movie you saw?
- Have you been on any interesting trips?
- What do you love about your job? or If you didn't have this job, what would be your passion job?
- Where would you go on vacation if you had no budget?
- Are you a dog or cat person?

Practice Activity

1. Videotape yourself during dinner.
   a. Are you taking small bites or large bites?
   b. Are you chewing with your mouth open or closed?
   c. Are you keeping your face neat?
   d. Are you talking with food in your mouth?
   e. Remember, it takes about two weeks to change a habit. You can also practice with your self-video until your new habits are consistent.
2. When you are eating with your family, ask them to give you a clue if you are reverting to old habits. You can decide on the clue. Sometimes just a stare is enough, sometimes a shaking of the head.
3. Practicing communication skills is something you can do every time you talk with someone.
   a. Maintain eye contact
   b. Listen to what others are saying.
   c. Practice asking a question for another to elaborate.
   d. Practice starting a conversation.
   e. It's good to ask your family to provide feedback so that you can improve this skill.

Cell Phone Etiquette

- Cell phones need be put on mute at the dinner table or during a discussion.
  - If you don't trust yourself not to play with the phone at dinner, leave it in your room or in the car.
  - Keep the phone off the table so that the people at the table know they are the priority. Putting your phone on the table subtly tells the others that whoever calls is more important. This is not helpful in making or keeping a friend.
- Emergency calls
  - It is rare that a text or call has to be answered immediately.
    - In the event that some people expect an immediate response, let them know that you will be at dinner, your phone will be on mute, and you will follow up later that day/evening.
  - If you need to keep your phone on for parents or children...
    - Let the other person know that you are keeping your phone on vibrate. You will need to check your phone, but you will not pick up for anyone else other than that person.

- If that person calls, and it is not an emergency, say that you will call them back after dinner.

- Response time
  - It is respectful to respond to someone who calls or texts you within a 24-hour period.
  - Generally, if someone calls or texts in the morning, it is polite to get back by the evening.
  - If the text or call is in the evening, the next day is fine.

However, if you are a procrastinator, respond as soon as possible so that you do not forget. Not responding sends the message you don't care or are disrespectful to the other person.

"Ghosting" is blocking all further communication on the cell phone without notice. The only time you should ghost is when the other person is behaving inappropriately, sexually, or rude. Otherwise, it is mean and immature. Anyone who ghosts you would not have made a good friend. This is not a loss.

If you reach out to someone and they do not respond after two attempts, stop texting. Try again in a week. If no response, you can try in a month. People do get busy and if you give them space, they may reach out or respond to a future text.

But if they still do not respond, stop texting. This person is not going to be your friend. There are so many people looking for friends, you just need to keep trying.

BE CAREFUL WHAT YOU SEND!
People who ask you to send nude photos are not friends. Once you send a picture, it can not be taken back. Your picture becomes the property of the other person and, in many states, they can do whatever they want with it. They can sell it; they can post it!

Social Media

If you would not want your mother to read or see it, it should not go on social media! Anything you put in print can be held against you.

Once you put something in writing it does not go away. Never say anything bad about others in writing, on cell phones, emails and social sites.

BEWARE
There are people on the internet eager to meet and take advantage of you. They look for people eager to make friends: cults , extreme political groups, sales scams and those engaging in illegal activities. They will be friendly, inviting, complement you and tell you how much they need you. These are NOT your friends.

Do not meet in person with anyone you met online, without telling someone with whom and where you are meeting. If you do meet, do it only in a public place. Do not get in their car! Predator's are smart and patient, It may take months before you really get to know who you are really meeting.

Finding Real Friends......

Make a list of all the things you like to do.
For example:
- Artwork or crafts
- Cooking/baking
- Watching movies or sports
- Participating in sports
- Listening to music
- Cycling, walking, hiking, fishing
- Anime
- Video Games

Find a group that engages in one of these activities.
- Search on the local recreation town website.
- Join a school club.
- Volunteer organizations are also great places to meet new friends.

You can ask a parent or friend to help you start a friend group with the guide "Creating a Friends Group".

Summary and Helpful Hints

Smile - People like to be around people who are happy and confident. It's harder to be anxious or sad when you have a smile on your face.

Dress the part - When you are dressed for success, you are much more likely to achieve success

Manage anxiety behaviors - It just takes awareness and practice!!

Eye Contact - Maintain eye contact when communicating, either as the speaker or the listener. If you notice the other person starts to lose eye contact, recognize this as boredom or disagreement. Change the topic or try to engage with a question.

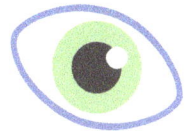

Join a group with people who have similar interests.

Making friends is a journey; an important journey that will increase your confidence and happiness. I am excited about your future! Making changes is always easiest among family and peers that like you, value you, and want to help you. It can be challenging to find a group that accepts you, within which you can practice and grow your confidence and skills. You just have to keep looking for the group that is right for you. Believe in yourself, be open to change, and practice.

If you have a relative who can help you create a friend group, there is another e-book that explains the process. It only takes a few people to create an instant group of friends. This also provides a safe space to practice and develop better social skills together. When people who want friends join together, they have friends. It's really that simple. When you are around true friends, anxiety reduces, motivation and processing increase, and change takes place much more easily and quickly. I believe this is the magic of having friends.

Wishing you friendship and happiness,
Sincerely,
Linda

www.ingramcontent.com/pod-product-compliance
Lightning Source LLC
Chambersburg PA
CBHW051249020426
42333CB00025B/3129